MORE THAN A BAND

DISCUSSIONS FOR WORSHIP TEAMS

GARY DURBIN

garydurbin.com

ISBN-13: 9798436136790

CONTENTS

FOR THE WORSHIP LEADER

I assume that if you're reading this chapter you are the worship leader, or leader of the worship team. Maybe there is more than one person who holds this responsibility or title. Maybe it's a joint leadership, which could be because you're in a really small church or a really large church. Being a worship leader is certainly not about a title. It's about leadership.

Whether you do this voluntarily, bi-vocationally, or full time, I want to thank you for the time and dedication you put into this ministry for the glory of God and good of your church. You are a blessing to your team and your church by providing the time, effort, and decision making that is needed. Stay humble and listen to any criticism that may come your way, but don't let it discourage you from serving the Lord and His church.

Please know that God is pleased with your faithfulness and please keep leading well and doing good. Galatians 6:9 encourages us to keep going and doing good, because the reward is coming as long as we don't give up. So, don't give up after that rough rehearsal or service. Don't give up when you have conflict with worship team members. Don't give up when you don't feel supported by the leadership at times. Keep going because the church needs you. Keep going because God is worthy and faithful. He's the one you serve and do this for. Being the worship leader is a big responsibility, but it's also a huge blessing. Enjoy it and encourage your team to enjoy it.

I hope this book is a help and blessing to you and your team as you serve your church. Make sure you take time to listen to your team as you discuss these topics. I've learned so much from my own team members by sitting down and listening to them talk about these things, and I want the same for you. If you have a small worship team, I recommend taking a few months and going through this book together.

If you have a rotation, it will take you a little longer to go through the material with everyone. This book could also be helpful on a getaway or retreat with your team. The first half of the book will examine your heart and your motives. The second half of the book focuses more on the practical side of things. I've written everything with an intentional broad scope. I would encourage you to include the tech team in these discussions as well. I believe if we do worship team ministry correctly, we will view and value everyone from the stage to the booth as part of our worship team.

Thank you for using this little book and investing in your team. Enjoy the journey and grow from it!

WHO IS THIS FOR?

Music is powerful. It can completely change the mood of a room and cue a reaction from a crowd. As people who provide the musical experience in worship each week, we understand this impact. A song can unite people in such a unique way, so when a church really starts to engage and lean in during our worship services, there's nothing truly more compelling to us than when we hear a room full of average singers lifting up praise to our God. That's what it's all about!

If that's what it's all about for you, then you're reading the right book. You may be a musician in front of the congregation, or you may be one of the brave souls behind them in the tech booth making sure that everything looks good and sounds good. This discussion is for people who desire to be a part of something more. Our churches deserve more than a band. They deserve more than a show. How we bring songs each and every week have a profound impact on what our church experiences. That's a huge responsibility and a humbling privilege.

Each section in the workbook is designed to help worship teams get better and be more than a band. Hopefully, this will be a group discussion with the whole team. Write down your answers to each question on your own and then come together as a worship team to discuss. Each chapter has three sections: **THE TEAM**, **THE CHURCH**, and **THE WORD**. **THE TEAM** section will challenge you to look in the mirror and see how you're doing as a worship team. **THE CHURCH** section will encourage you to think about your congregation and how you can help them worship. **THE WORD** section focuses on what God thinks based on a passage of scripture.

At the end of each chapter there is a very important section called **NOW WHAT?** Allow that to be a time of confession, application, and celebration. Don't let pride get in the way of your individual growth or team growth. My prayer is that these discussions will help cultivate some conversations on your team and bring unity in how we lead our church in worship.

CHAPTER ONE

WHAT IS MORE?

A.W. Tozer said, *"The church that can't worship must be entertained. And the men who can't lead a church to worship must provide the entertainment."* When we think of the word MORE, too often we're conditioned to think of bigger and better. Unfortunately, this has translated into entertaining congregations instead of engaging them in worship. Entertainment in church services is often justified as an evangelistic mission of the church. The danger in this approach is we can start believing that God needs our creativity. He has given us the gift of His Son and His Word, which is truly all that is needed for salvation and redemption. If we're not careful, we start thinking we need more. But what is more? Is there anything more powerful than God's presence? Have you heard any dialogue that is more life changing than His Word? The answer is simple: He is MORE!

We live in a society that is looking for more. When life is hard, people hope that there is more than all of what we see and experience. As believers in Jesus Christ, we know the Good News! There is more, and Jesus is more. Because we are involved in leading worship in our services, we get to point people to more.

DISCUSSION QUESTIONS

the TEAM

When we think of being more than a band, let's think in terms of impact instead of entertainment. Entertainment is a tempting motive, whether you're in the tech booth or on the stage, but there is more.

How would you define entertainment in a church setting?

How would you define impact?

Am I ever tempted to entertain instead of impact? Why or why not?

the CHURCH

In this time and culture of the local church, there is a very high expectation for excellence in corporate worship. Large churches have raised the bar in worship arts for their church goers. As a result, congregants of smaller churches are exposed to the high-quality production that mega churches are bringing every week. If we're not careful, this can bring an unhealthy demand for more entertainment and a lack of participation.

What are some good reasons to have a high standard of excellence in our worship services?

What are signs that high quality production has become an unhealthy demand in our church?

List out characteristics of a congregation that is engaged, instead of entertained.

the WORD

Read Colossians 2:16-17. Paul speaks into the importance of not putting too much focus on the methods of our worship. This is a challenge at times for us who have to focus on playing songs and running tech with excellence.

What are some specific methods we put too much faith in?

According to Colossians 2:16-17, who is the substance of our worship?

What are some consequences of losing our focus on Christ in our worship?

What are some benefits of keeping our focus on Christ in our worship?

NOW WHAT?

In light of what has been discussed…

What changes do you need to make personally?

How can we improve in this area as a team?

What are we already getting right in this area?

CHAPTER TWO

TALENT AND HEART

Many people find it appealing to serve on the worship team. Whether it be singing, playing an instrument, or running sound, you get to be a part of the most visible aspect of the worship service. While many people would like to serve in worship ministry, not everyone is meant to do so. You could say the same thing about all ministries. God has gifted and geared us all in specific ways, and those leanings help us find our place. For worship ministry, there's obviously a need for musical and technical talent. That's why most ministries have an audition process. In fact, every worship team, no matter the size of the ministry, should have some sort of audition process. It's much more difficult and painful to remove someone rather than telling them no in an audition. Auditions are not done out of pride or arrogance. They are a way to recognize talent. If done properly, they are also a way to recognize heart. Andy Stanley says, *"Your talent and giftedness as a leader have the potential to take you farther than your character can sustain you."*

It's one thing to have the talent to be on the team, but it's also crucial to have the same heart for the ministry. This heart and mindset will reveal itself in the chemistry dynamic of your team. For church worship teams, one way to ensure this is to require everyone to become a member of the church before they are added to the team.

Not every church has a membership process, so in those cases, make sure you have conversations regarding unity and commitment. Serving on a worship team should not be looked at as a gig. It should be more than a gig, and we should be more than a band. We are brothers and sisters in Christ who are in community, serving Jesus together. Each member is using the gifts He has given to us. It's important to have talent, but our heart will be what sustains us. When a worship team has both talent and heart, it makes for a beautiful tapestry of service to God and His ministry.

DISCUSSION QUESTIONS

the TEAM

Talent is important, but if Andy Stanley is correct, it should be concerning to us that our talent could potentially lead us astray. God has gifted us and geared us to serve Him with humility. If we allow pride to seep into our hearts, we are obviously missing the mark in worship.

Why is talent important to our worship team?

What does it look like to use our talents with humility?

How can we guard against pride as we serve on this team?

the CHURCH

Sharing the same heartbeat as the church or ministry we serve in is something that should not be overlooked or neglected. Psalm 133 talks about how much God loves unity. It's important that we have a heart to serve our church, otherwise we will just be serving ourselves.

List some specific characteristics that describe the heart of our church.

What are the dangers of a worship team not sharing the same heartbeat as their church?

What does it look like when a worship team serves the church instead of themselves?

the WORD

Read Psalm 33:3. Notice the command to play *"skillfully."*

Why do you think that the Bible asks for skill when it comes to playing music?

Read Psalm 139:1 and Proverbs 16:2.

How should the knowledge of these scriptures affect the way we serve?

What are some ways we can achieve a healthy balance of talent and heart on our team?

NOW WHAT?

In light of what has been discussed…

What changes do you need to make personally?

How can we improve in this area as a team?

What are we already getting right in this area?

CHAPTER THREE

THE WHAT

As a collection of singers, instrumentalists, and technicians, we can be very creative together. The possibilities of songs, videos, and light presentations are virtually endless, depending on your set up. There is a lot we can do, but just because we CAN does not always mean we SHOULD. This leads us to a very monumental question: *What should we do?*

Naturally, there's going to be a lot of opinions and strong feelings about the answer to that question. But whenever I think of what God wants, it all comes back to worship. That's what He's seeking and longing for. In fact, He's jealous for our worship. In our context, the WHAT is CORPORATE WORSHIP. What greater privilege do we have as a worship team than to lead our church to worship the Father each and every week? Unfortunately, we sometimes trade the greater for the lesser. In the context of a church service, corporate worship is that greater thing. There is great power when we gather together to exalt Christ. Hearts are softened and broken for God's voice and calling. Lives are changed when the focus is put on our Redeemer and His Word. Corporate, responsive worship is way more impactful than a cover song for the sake of cultural relevance. I'm not suggesting that covering a Top 40 song is wrong, but if we really believe that we need to do those things for evangelism, then we may need to check our belief in the power of the Gospel. Corporate worship is truly incomparable in our services, and it's the unique practice that you can only find in the gathering of believers. I'll even go as far as saying that it's one of the most evangelistic tools we have. Corporate worship is that "more" that people are often looking for. It's what makes us more than just a band. Why would we settle for anything less?

DISCUSSION QUESTIONS

the TEAM

There's so much we can accomplish with the talent that God has given us, and there's truly no greater accomplishment than inspiring others to worship Jesus. This is an incredible opportunity and mission.

Define corporate worship in your own words.

What are some reasons we should be continually excited about the opportunity of corporate worship?

If corporate worship is the greater thing, what are some lesser things we can settle for?

the CHURCH

The people we lead every week live in the same broken and fallen world we live in. Believers are looking to respond in worship, and those who are far from God are simply looking for more. Our mission is to point them to Jesus, because He is the answer, and He is more.

What specific ways do, or can we give our congregation to respond in corporate worship?

How can corporate worship be an evangelistic tool?

What are some things that battle the congregation's focus on Jesus in corporate worship?

the WORD

Read John 4:23. When it comes to worship, it's vital that we ask what God wants.

What does it mean to worship God in spirit and truth?

Read Romans 12:1.

How does corporate worship help us offer our bodies as living sacrifices?

NOW WHAT?

In light of what has been discussed…

What changes do you need to make personally?

How can we improve in this area as a team?

What are we already getting right in this area?

CHAPTER FOUR

THE WHY

If our mission is to point people to Jesus in corporate worship, then what is our motive? If corporate worship is the WHAT, then what is the WHY? Getting this right is huge. *It is possible to do the right things for the wrong reasons.* That's a scary truth that we need to be aware of as we serve. At the conclusion of the Gospel of John, Jesus repeatedly asked Peter if he loved Him. Every time Peter said *"yes,"* Jesus continually commissioned him to serve His flock. Jesus correlates serving with loving. The WHAT and the WHY are closely connected. Our mission must be accompanied by the right motive, or else we work in vain.

In I Samuel 16, God told Samuel that even though people judge based on the outward appearance, He looks straight to the heart and motive. God wants us to be doers, but He is equally as concerned with *why* we are doing something. In Matthew 22, Jesus gives us the clear-cut, simple answer to the longstanding question of WHY. We must love God and we must love people. We serve because we love. Adversely, when our motives are out of line, our selfishness and pride will kick in, which will lead to an eventual fall. This obviously is of no help to God and His church, and it certainly is not in our own best interest. One habit I've created is to pray before every worship service. I pray specific prayers with our team. One prayer I've repeated with our team is that the congregation will see God as soon as possible. Pride keeps us in a secret prayer that everyone will see us and be impressed with what we can do. Pride is ugly, but praise is beautiful. Our mission and motive is to be like Jesus and to radiate the glory of God in corporate worship. When others question your motives, let that always be the answer.

DISCUSSION QUESTIONS

the TEAM

Serving on a worship team can be a great test of heart and motivation. With all of the production and attention, it's very easy to forget the WHY.

What are some indicators that pride, instead of praise, has become our motivation as we serve?

In the role in which you serve, what are some of the right things you do that can be done for the wrong reasons? Explain.

How can we use production to give God all of the glory?

the CHURCH

Worship ministry is not just the music portion of the service. It's actually more. Our songs play a part of the discipleship process for our church, and the way in which we present those songs can point people toward Jesus or ourselves.

What does it look like when our congregation sees God as soon as possible in our services?

When our motives are out of line, what kind of effects can that have on our church?

If we were to survey our church about our motives, what kind of things would they say?

the WORD

Read Matthew 22:34-40.

As a worship team, what are specific ways we can love God?

What are specific ways we can love our congregation each week?

NOW WHAT?

In light of what has been discussed…

What changes do you need to make personally?

How can we improve in this area as a team?

What are we already getting right in this area?

CHAPTER FIVE
MORE WE THAN ME

When it's done right, a worship team is more than a team and more than a band. We are a family. We are the church. We are brothers and sisters in Christ who happen to utilize our gifts in the areas of worship arts. Everyone contributes in their own unique way. There are different personalities that need to work together and co-exist, but we do it all with a heart to serve.

On the flip side, if it's done wrong, a worship team is going to have issues. If there's a brother or sister in Christ on the team that has their heart in the wrong place, it can affect the rest of the team. We are each, individually, a vital body part. Whether you play an instrument, run tech, or hold a microphone, each individual has a role that can dramatically impact the effectiveness of the team. You can also impact the chemistry of the team.

The attitude and spirit that you serve with can affect the vibe and mood of rehearsals, sound checks, and services. We all love to be around people who are team players and put others before themselves. The flip side are those who allow their pride and ego to take over, which results in *self-centeredness* and even a *territorial spirit,* both of which can negatively affect the team. *Self-centeredness* often manifests itself with a selfish agenda. Maybe the worship leader isn't putting you in the spot you want. Maybe you don't like the song selection. Self-centeredness can easily derail us and cause us to hurt the chemistry of our team. A *territorial spirit* breathes life into the pride in our heart. Instead of celebrating team growth, you feel threatened by new talent coming on the rotation.

What we need to do is zoom out to see the big picture. We need to humble ourselves and think less about what we want. We need to own the team more than our position. We do this when we let go of the exhaustion of self-centeredness and embrace the exhilaration of empowering others as they use their gifts for the Kingdom. What I'm suggesting is that we think more WE than ME. When we do this, we put others before ourselves and truly serve with our God-given talents. Basically, when we think more WE than ME, we are more like Jesus…the ultimate worship leader.

DISCUSSION QUESTIONS

the TEAM

When we think more WE than ME, the culture of our worship team will be healthy. Healthy teams will inevitably grow. We will grow spiritually as we humble ourselves. We will also grow numerically in our rotation and experience fresh ideas as new talent comes on board.

How can we battle a self-centered spirit even when we don't agree with decisions made?

What does it mean to own the team more than the position?

What are some indicators of a healthy, selfless culture on a worship team?

the CHURCH

A more WE than ME culture will be evident and beneficial to our church family. A humble spirit in serving and a steady rotation models selflessness in worship for our church.

What are some practical ways we can model humility for our congregation?

When we have a steady rotation on our team, what kind of message does that send to our church family?

What does selflessness look like in the context of corporate worship?

the WORD

Read Romans 12:4-5 and 1 Corinthians 12:12.

What is your function and part in the body of the worship team?

What does it mean to be “many, but one body?"

NOW WHAT?

In light of what has been discussed…

What changes do you need to make personally?

How can we improve in this area as a team?

What are we already getting right in this area?

CHAPTER SIX
IMPROVING YOUR SKILL

Whether you serve in the tech booth or on stage, you're on the worship team because you have a specific skill. It's ok to agree with that, as long you give God the credit. He is the one who has given you the talent and skill. Using it to serve the church means you're giving it back to Him as an offering of praise. Another way to honor Him is to improve your talent and skill. No one who has a specific skillset was born with an advanced skill level. When you get better, the team gets better, and the church reaps the benefit.

Just like anything else, to get better, you have to put in the work. We live in a time of much access. Because of the internet, we have access to countless self-improvement tools, so, we have very little excuse. Time is the other variable. I know with my schedule it's easy not to prioritize self-improvement, but if I want to get better, I need to WANT to get better. If I want it bad enough, it will be a priority. I will make the time. Another thing I've learned is that some of the best resources are the people on my team. There's always going to be someone better than you, and that someone may already be on your team. It's ok to admit that and to benefit from them. Pride is an ugly weight that will hold you back and hold you down. Take advantage of the relationships that God has put right in front of you and learn from those around you. One thing our worship team has done to help everyone in this area is occasional workshops. I've empowered people on our team to find resources in order to teach and invest in helping other team members grow in their craft. About once a quarter, we cancel our rehearsal night and facilitate workshops at our church building. Once we started this, we instantly saw relational and spiritual growth, and we also watched the bar raise on our skill level. Empowering team members to lead has been a freeing and beneficial move for my team, especially for me. It's freed me up to lead the big picture of things, and the ones who are leading the workshops are doing a better job than I would at focusing in on the things that will improve the specific and unique skillsets of our team members. The planning and execution of these workshops is very important, but the key to its success is reliant on the humility of our team. As long as we stay humble and understand the need for improving our skill, we will get better, individually and as a team.

DISCUSSION QUESTIONS

the TEAM

Michael Jordan once said, *"Everybody has talent, but ability takes hard work."* There are always going to be different skill levels on every team, but we all have the same opportunity to work hard and improve our skill. We all have room to improve. Our pride is the only thing that will hold us back in this area. Humility will drive us to always get better and learn from each other.

On a scale of 1-10, how would you rate your priority level when it comes to improving your skill? Explain.

What are some signs that pride is hindering you from improving your skill?

What are some specific steps we can take to develop a culture of learning, growing, and helping each other improve?

the CHURCH

When our skill level as a team improves, our church will benefit from it. If the quality of the music and production is low, it will be something that our congregation has to overlook and overcome as they worship. God is certainly bigger than our skill. We should be able to worship, no matter how bad the quality is. That said, if we can improve and do better, why not do so? Let's serve God to the best of our ability. It's not about impressing our church. It's about blessing our church.

How will our church benefit from us improving our skill level, as a team?

What are some of the distractions our congregations face when the quality is low?

What's the difference between impressing our church and blessing our church?

the WORD

Read Psalm 33:3. Notice the command to play "skillfully."

Why do you think that the Bible asks for skill when it comes to playing music?

Read James 4:10

What kind of effect can humility have on me improving my skill?

NOW WHAT?

In light of what has been discussed…

What changes do you need to make personally?

How can we improve in this area as a team?

What are we already getting right in this area?

CHAPTER SEVEN

PRACTICE ON YOUR OWN

These next two chapters should be helpful in clarifying the difference between *practice* and *rehearsal*. Those terms are often used interchangeably, but there is a huge difference. Years ago, a wise church leader shared with me that *practice is what you do on your own, and rehearsal is what you do when you come together.* It's a very clear, simple, and successful concept. When we practice well, we will rehearse well. This formula produces only good results, including the quality of what we do in our worship services. When you practice on your own it shows that you care about those results, and it shows that you care about the church you serve. It also says that you are serving with excellence. When we serve with excellence, we are serving with the biblical concept of doing everything with the intention of representing Jesus well. Another result is a happy team, especially the worship leader.

As a worship leader, I can tell you that when my team practices on their own, it can dramatically affect my week. When my team doesn't put in the work and own their part, it makes me work harder. When team members come in practiced and prepared, it allows me to focus less on the music and more on the shepherding aspect of the worship set. When you practice, it will also allow you to enjoy serving that week. It's hard to have fun in the moment when you're not prepared. When you and your team are having fun during the worship service, it's a testimony of excellence. Practice is something that can easily get neglected. Some of us are talented enough to show up at rehearsal and do our part without preparation. That can become a bad habit and limit your ability. Some of us are lucky just to be able to make it to a rehearsal or worship service some weeks. My challenge to you would be to make serving with excellence a priority as much as possible. Most of us can improve our time management and find areas to adjust, so let's do that.

Most churches provide online tools for practice. Utilize those as you practice on your own. This can apply to those who are in the tech or on the stage. Take the time to really learn your part and really learn the songs. When you internalize the experience privately, you will enjoy the experience publicly so much more.

DISCUSSION QUESTIONS

the TEAM

We have all been a part of a team where not everyone practices the same. Maybe you could improve in this area. Practicing on our own will always affect the rest of the team. When you practice, you're not only improving what you do, you're improving the vibe of a rehearsal and worship service.

What are some bad excuses not to practice on the week you serve? What are some good excuses?

How does a lack of individual practice negatively affect our team? What are the positive results of practice?

In my specific position, how can I best utilize the tools I've been given to practice?

the CHURCH

Practicing is an individual issue. As an individual, you represent the excellence of the team to the church by the way you serve, whether that be during a worship service or in fellowship with our church family.

Based on the way in which I serve, how would my church rate the excellence level and culture of our team? Explain.

What does it mean to represent excellence during a worship service and in fellowship with our church family?

What's the correlation between practicing on your own and caring for your church?

the WORD

Read Colossians 3:16-17.

How does practicing on your own represent our Lord Jesus?

What kind of effect does thankfulness have on our priority to practice?

NOW WHAT?

In light of what has been discussed…

What changes do you need to make personally?

How can we improve in this area as a team?

What are we already getting right in this area?

CHAPTER EIGHT
REHEARSE TOGETHER

Every production has a similar formula. Everyone involved has a part to play. Team members work and prepare, then they get together for a big dress rehearsal before they present it before the crowds. These rehearsals are vital. They reveal the areas that need to be polished up. Worship team rehearsals should have the same function. It's not a time to learn songs. It's a time to polish songs.

Remember that practice is what you do on your own, and rehearsal is what you do when you come together. It's an opportunity for unity and getting on the same page as a team, musically and spiritually. Think of rehearsals with a two-fold goal in mind: play together and pray together. First, we need to learn to play together, which is the musical and technical side of things. We've all individually practiced and learned our part. Rehearsal is the moment we can combine our contributions and experience chemistry. It's not enough for you to know and play your part. You need to play your part in cohesiveness with your teammates. That's called chemistry and it can't be overstated in its importance. Usually, once every rehearsal, I will say, "play together" as we're in the middle of a song. My team knows that I'm referring to chemistry. To play together, it requires everyone to listen to each other, and in turn, play off one another. Chemistry in the tech booth requires great communication between the positions. There's specific cues and slides that work together. When the tech team has great communication, the lighting, slides, and sound have a cohesion that enhances the worship experience in an impactful way.

Second, we need to learn to pray together, which is the spiritual side of things. The Bible says that we need the Spirit in order to proclaim our worship to Christ. When we gather to pray before and after we play, we're inviting God into our rehearsal. Prayer is our opportunity to talk to God and ask for His favor on our efforts. It's an opportunity to pray for each other and pray for our church. In many ways, prayer is that moment of perspective we so desperately need. We pray together to remember WHY we play together. Rehearsals are truly essential in growing and serving as a team. Make the most of them!

DISCUSSION QUESTIONS

the TEAM

Rehearsals should be a priority for every team member. When we rehearse with each other with chemistry as a goal, we'll listen to each other and work together. These kinds of rehearsals produce better teams and a fun environment.

In your own words, what does it mean to play together?

What are the signs of lack of chemistry?

How does praying together at rehearsals help our chemistry?

the CHURCH

Great rehearsals lead to great worship services. The chemistry we have as a team will help us focus on leading the congregation in spiritual aspects, as well as the musical and technical.

Why does chemistry free us up to focus on the spiritual aspect of leading worship?

How does chemistry in the musical and technical aspects help our congregation worship?

How can we specifically pray for our congregation at rehearsals?

the WORD

Read 1 Corinthians 12:3.

What does "in the Spirit" mean?

How can we proclaim the Lordship of Christ in our rehearsals?

NOW WHAT?

In light of what has been discussed…

What changes do you need to make personally?

How can we improve in this area as a team?

What are we already getting right in this area?

CHAPTER NINE
WORSHIP ALWAYS

Worship is almost synonymous with music. We say that it's bigger than music, but when we ask people to sing together, we usually ask them to join us in a time of *worship*. That is not incorrect. If we're doing it correctly, we should be worshipping God when we sing in church. The big mistake is when we minimize worship to the singing time of a church service.

Worship is a broad topic that is active in every area of our life. It's not a question of *if* we worship, but *who* or *what* we worship. As a worship team, our given context is that our worship is directed to God and God alone. When we think of that in a broad sense, worship will go beyond a song or a service. For us, it must go beyond the performance. Too often, we can rely on how we serve on the team for our worship.

Over the course of my ministry, I've had team members occasionally drop out of church as soon as their position or place of service was minimized. This shows that their worship is entirely too dependent on their serving. When we truly love God with all of our being, serving will only be a part of how we worship God. We don't worship because we serve. We serve because we worship. I had a worship leader once tell me that they worship God most when they're on the stage. Think about how minimal that is. What if you only loved your friends and family for 15-20 minutes a week and only at a certain time? Love and worship must be a daily dedication to God. My challenge for us that have the privilege to be on a worship team is to worship always. On the weeks you're not on rotation, do you still worship with the same passion? If not, take that to heart and find out why. That needs to change. When you learn to fully worship off stage or out of the tech booth, you will more fully worship when you serve with your talent.

All that said, let's not forget to worship *when we serve*. There's nothing more contagious or catalytic as when those who are leading in worship lead in worship. We can easily get too consumed with the production and the performance and completely forget about the praise. I'm also thinking of the tech team. Sometimes my tech team actually leads me in worship when I look back there and see them engaged and expressing their worship to God. Simply put, don't forget to worship. Whether you are on stage, in the tech booth, or in the congregation, worship God always. It's the least we can do for the lover of our soul.

DISCUSSION QUESTIONS

the TEAM

A common trap we can fall into is contextualizing our worship to how or when we serve. When we do that, we put conditions on when we worship, if we're not careful. When we worship always, we are saying that we love God no matter the setting or situation. When we don't, we are saying something else.

When we contextualize and limit our worship to God only when we serve, what are we saying?

What is my biggest challenge to worship always when I serve? What about when I am not serving in rotation?

What are some clear characteristics of a team that worships always?

the CHURCH

Worship is contagious. Much like a virus, the only way we can give it to someone is if we have it ourselves. When we lead in worship, whether we're serving or not, our church will take notice and follow. They will be inspired to worship.

What are some tangible indicators to our church that our team has love and worship for God?

Do you think our church can tell if our worship is authentic or not? Explain.

How can I lead in worship when I'm in the congregation with my church?

the WORD

Read Psalm 34:1.

The phrase "all times" is pretty clear. If I were to worship God always, how would my life look different?

What does it mean for God's praise to continually be in my mouth?

NOW WHAT?

In light of what has been discussed…

What changes do you need to make personally?

How can we improve in this area as a team?

What are we already getting right in this area?

BOOK FOR WORSHIP LEADERS

available at
amazon

ABOUT THE AUTHOR

Gary Durbin has been a worship leader in the church since 2002. Gary is also a songwriter and is passionate about serving the local church. He has written and recorded several songs that are predominantly geared for corporate worship. In 2015, he recorded and released "Almighty" which received national attention. In 2017, he published his first book called ***More Than a Worship Leader***, which is available on Amazon.

Gary is available for events to lead worship, speak, or teach workshops.

For more information go to:

garydurbin.com

NOTES

NOTES

NOTES

Made in United States
Orlando, FL
19 December 2024

56214041R00048